LEARNING TO SEE

WHAT A

CHILD'S HANDWRITING

SHOWS AND TELLS

EDITH NAMM, M.A.,C.G.S.

Specialized Handwriting Analyst

AuthorHouse™
1663 Liberty Drive, Suite 200
Bloomington, IN 47403
www.authorhouse.com
Phone: 1-800-839-8640

First published by AuthorHouse 02/01/2008

ISBN: 978-1-5850-0053-1 (sc)

Printed in the United States of America
Bloomington, Indiana
This book is printed on acid-free paper.

Dear Reader,

My goal is to take you on an exciting journey to discover:

– The basic concepts of handwriting analysis that show you how to identify the signs of anger, fear, and depression in a child's handwriting.

– Simple Script — a positive primary learning experience.

– The "write" way for pre-teens and adolescents to relieve feelings of anger, fear, and sadness.

– PEP (Positive Energy Power) Aerobics — the handwritten exercises that can empower children to feel self-confident, set realistic, achievable goals and increase their smile mileage.

Planning and preparing the road map for your journey has been an exciting and rewarding experience for me. I welcome you aboard. Travel at a speed that is comfortable for you. Travel with the confidence of knowing that your journey will empower you to teach children the "write" way to increase their positive energy power, experience a positive state of well-being and successfully cope with the daily stress of living in a hectic ever-changing world.

Enjoy your journey to positive energy power.

Wishing you miles of smiles - today, tomorrow and always.

Edith Namm

Websites: www.enamm.com

www.share-a-smile-ambassadors.com

Road Map To *See What A Child's Handwriting Shows and Tells*

THE WRITE WAY TO FEEL GOOD ABOUT YOURSELF
A GUIDE TO EMPOWER A PRE-TEEN/ ADOLESCENT
TO SUCCESSFULLY COPE WITH THE STRESS OF
DAILY LIVING

Graphology A Brief History

--Graphology is a reliable, unbiased scientific system of personality assessment through the study of a Person's Handwriting.

--Graphology is not a new science.

--The Chinese noted a relationship between Handwriting, Character, and Personality as early as the 11th century.

--In 1622, Camillo Baldi, Doctor and Professor at the University of Bologna, wrote the oldest published book on the subject of Graphology. *How To Judge The Nature and The Character of a Person From His Letter.*

--*Ideographia* by Alderisius Prosper, published in Bologna in the beginning of the 17th century, identified the relationship between Handwriting Traits and Character Traits.

--In the 1870's, French Priests, Abbe Flandria, and Abbe Jean-Hypolyte Michon (known as the Founder of European Graphology) published writing in which they referred to Graphology as the art of knowing men by their Handwriting.

--Ludwig Klages, well-known German Philosopher, established Laws and Principles of Graphology during the late 1800's and early 1900's.

--Sigmund Freud published information about the validity and use of Graphology.

--Alfred Binet, Inventor of the IQ test, referred to Graphology as the "Science of the Future"

--Milton Bunker, in his intensive, methodical research from 1915 - 1929, discovered the importance of the Handwriting Stroke, identified over 100 Personality Traits in Handwriting, and founded the International Graphoanalysis Society and School in Chicago, Illinois.

The Research Behind The Concept: An Individual's Personality Traits Can Be Changed By Changing The Individual's Handwriting.

--Between 1929 and 1931, The Concept was clinically tested at the Sorbonne by French psychologist Professor Charles Henry and physician Dr. Pierre Janet. The results achieved were positive and impressive.

--In 1931, Dr. Pierre Menard, a distinguished psychology professor, lecturer, and author of many books and articles on Medicine and Psychology, put the tested Concept into practice. His success in positively modifying children's behavior by changing their handwriting won the support of doctors, psychologists, and teachers.

--Based upon 25 years of extensive research, noted Graphologist, Paul de Sainte Columbe, in his book _Grapho-Therapeutics_, published in 1966, claimed success in using handwriting changes to bring about personality improvements.

--Dr. Richard J. Stoller, in his book, _Write Right: Change Your Writing to Change Your Life_, published in 1977, showed that, by incorporating positive trait strokes into a Child's handwriting, negative attitudes and a poor self-image can be changed. The Concept, used in both individual and group settings, proved to be effective in approximately 80% of the cases.

THE GRAPHO TRAIT DETECTORS THAT SHOW AND TELL
A WRITER'S PERSONALITY TRAITS AND EMOTIONAL STATE OF MIND
AT THE TIME THE SYMBOLS ARE PLACED ON THE PAPER

-- Overall Organization
   -- Spacing
   -- Rhythm
   -- Legibility

-- Slant

-- Pressure

-- Letter Size

-- Baseline

Emotions Affect The Rhythm Of Finger Muscle Movements.

---Finger action is controlled by two sets of Flexor Muscles -- the Extensors and the Retractors.

---The Extensor Muscles extend the fingers to form upward strokes and rightward movements-- rounded relaxed formations.

---The Retractor Muscles contract the fingers to form downward strokes, leftward movements,- straight and angular formations.

---Steady rhythmic contraction and release movements across the page indicate the Extensor and Retractor Muscles are operating in harmony with each other. The Writer is in harmony with self and surroundings.

---Graphically Expressed
--Smooth, continuous flow of contraction and release movements.
--Consistency in Baseline, Slant, Letter Size, Pressure, and Stroke Formation.
--Balanced Spacing between Words, Letters, and Lines.

---Anger, Fear, and Anxiety disrupt rhythmic muscle functioning. Retractor Muscles remain taut and tense and prevent the Extensor Muscle Release Movement.

---Graphically Expressed
--Inconsistency in Slant, letter Size, Pressure, and Stroke Formation.
--Descending, irregular Baseline.
--Angular, narrow letter formations, frequent breaks within words, retraced loops, closely spaced words, crowded letters, overlapping lines of writing, reflect Tension, Irritability, Confusion.
The Writer is experiencing difficulty in coping and expressing his/her Fears.

Does Your" Slant On Life -Tend To Lean To The Right Or To The Left?
Do You Tend To Look Forward To The Future Or Look Back On The Past?

The Slant of Letter Strokes -- The Emotional Foundation
of Personality

---In Handwriting, the Slant of Upstroke Letters determines the degree of Emotional Response to
environment, people, and the future.

---The degree of Emotional Response is
--determined by the direction in which the Upstroke Letters lean Rightward, Leftward
or are Vertical.
--based upon emotionally positive or negative experiences in Childhood.

---Direction is symbolically expressed in Handwriting.
--A Rightward Direction symbolizes the future and interaction with people.
--A Leftward Direction symbolizes the past - withdrawal from social interaction, and
the uncertainties of the future.

---To determine Slant Direction, measure the upstroke of upper zone letters
b, h, k, l
--Draw a Baseline under the letter to be measured.
--Draw a dot where the Upstroke leaves the Baseline.
--Place a dot where the Upstroke stops going in an upward direction.
--Connect the two dots.
--For an adequate sampling of Slant Direction, measure at least 50 consecutive
Upstrokes.
--Concentrate on Upstrokes in the mid-portion of the script.
--Tally the number of Rightward, Leftward, and Vertical Slants to determine the
predominant Emotional Pattern.

SLANT DIAGRAM

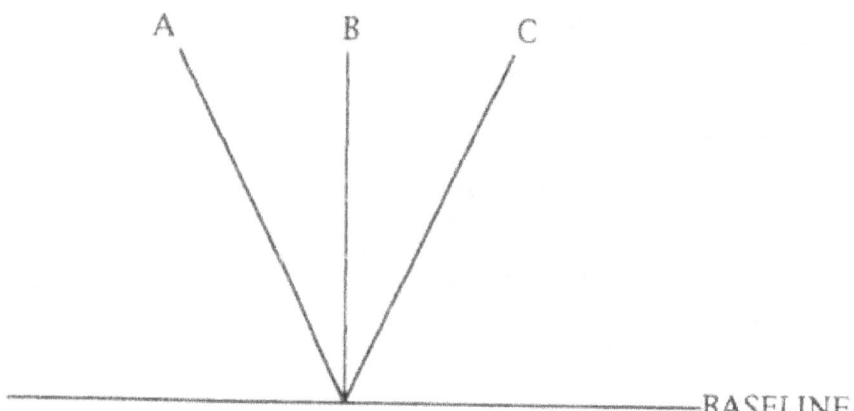

A -- Left Slant Leans Back To The Left.

B -- Vertical Slant Stands Straight Up And Down.

C -- Right Slant Leans Forward To The Right.

LEFT SLANT   VERTICAL SLANT   RIGHT SLANT

---The Rightward Slant -- The Extroverted Personality
--The Rightward Slant reflects a Writer who

--is future oriented--eagerly anticipates events to come.

--is friendly, sociable, warm, affectionate.

--The Extreme Rightward Slant reflects a Writer who

--is overexcited, overinvolved, overstimulated, oversensitive.

--is excessively expressive and impulsive,

--is insecure, jealous, nervous, dependent on others for ego support.

--is easily frustrated and exhausted as a result of the high degree of emotional involvement and restlessness.

--makes decisions based on feelings rather than on facts.

--has wide mood swings, emotional outbursts.

--has strong likes and dislikes.

---The Leftward Slant -- The Introverted Personality
--The Leftward Slant reflects a Writer who

--is self-oriented, inhibited, reserved, indecisive, cautious, insecure, impersonal, undemonstrative.

--The Extreme Leftward Slant reflects a Writer who

--feels lonely and isolated.

--fears establishing trusting relationships as a result of previous emotional trauma.

--withdraws to avoid possible future painful situation.

---The Vertical Slant -- The Level-Headed Personality

    --The Vertical Slant reflects a Writer who

        --is sensible, logical, realistic, independent .analytical, disciplined,
            undemonstrative, objective in judgments.

        --appears calm ,reserved, and poised.

---The Variable Slant --The Conflicted Personality

    --The Variable Slant is a combination of two or three slants within any 10 consecutive
        letters in a writing sample.

    --The Variable Slant reflects a Writer who

        --is pulled in all directions.

        --is confused, inconsistent, indecisive, unpredictable, unreliable, undisciplined,
            nervous, excitable, belligerent, defiant, rebellious.

        --has had unhappy early life experiences as a result of conflict between male and
            female authority figures.

IMPORTANT NOTE:

---<u>Never</u> attempt to change, correct, or criticize an Individual's Writing Slant.

---The Writing Slant reflects an Individual's basic Emotional
        Temperament --the core of his/her Personality.

---Slant changes can be noted when a Writer experiences an
        emotionally traumatic event.

How Can You Accurately Determine Your Level Of Vitality And Energy?

Pen Pressure (Heavy, moderate, or light)

---How lightly or heavily a Writer presses on a ball point pen, at the time of writing, accurately reveals
    --vitality, will power, and health.
    --emotional response intensity.

---Moderately heavy Pressure, represented by firm, dark, thick pen stokes, reflects a Writer who
    --is energetic, ambitious, assertive, determined and in good physical health.
    --has a retentive memory.

---Light Pressure, represented by fine, thin, light, pen strokes, reflects a Writer who
    --is gentle, calm, passive, sensitive, timid, anxious, impressionable, easily influenced.
    --lacks physical energy, vitality, determination, confidence, self assurance
    --easily forgets and forgives, resists commitments.

---RED ALERT!!!

---Extremely heavy, strong Pressure, represented by very dark, thick pen stokes and
    deep impressions on the back of the paper, reflects a Writer who
  --is tense, easily frustrated, explosive, aggressive, fearful, stubborn.
  --over reacts to emotionally charged situations.
  --has intense feelings of anger, fear, love, hate, and anxiety.
  --harbors grudges, dwells on past events, resists change.

---Extremely light Pressure reflects a Writer who
  --is overly timid, submissive, insecure, anxious, physically weak.
  --lacks will power.

---Variable, uneven Pressure Patterns (word to word - letter to letter) reflects a Writer
  who
  --is indecisive, impatient, restless, irritable, frustrated, angry, nervous, unreliable, unable to
    cope.

---Interesting Note:

  --Heavy Pressure Writers prefer bright, intense, warm colors -red, orange, yellow.

  --Light Pressure Writers prefer pastels, cool colors - blue and green.

One Size Does Not Fit All!

Middle Zone Letter Size (Average, Large, Small)

---The Size of Middle Zone Letters reveals
--how a Writer relates to his environment.
--a Writer's capacity for concentration.

---Average Middle Zone Letter Size reveals a Writer who
--is adaptable, reliable, socially well-balanced.
--has average ability to concentrate.

---Large Middle Zone Letter Size (1/4" or larger) reveals a Writer who
--is extroverted, people and action oriented, outgoing, outspoken, energetic.
--has a need to be noticed.
--seeks recognition and approval of others.
--is concerned with generalities rather than specifics.
--is unwilling to concentrate on small details or be confined to a limited area of space.

---Small Middle Zone Letter Size (1/16" or smaller) reveals
a Writer who
--is introverted, withdrawn, timid, cautious, analytical, precise, attentive to details,
        detached from external stimuli - people, objects, events.
--has a high level of concentration, a narrow scope of interest.
--blocks out all distractions, concentrates on one thing at a time.
--avoids close relationships.

RED ALERT !!!

---**Exaggerated and extremely large Middle Zone Size Letters** reflect a Writer who is
--obsessed with an exaggerated need for attention.
--demonstrates excessive restlessness, vitality, and hyperactivity.

---**Overly small, microscopic, illegible Middle Zone Letters** reflect a Writer who is
--withdrawn, fearful, indecisive, narrow-minded, emotionally, physically, and
intellectually removed from human interaction.

---**Inconsistencies in height, width, and spacing of Middle Zone Letters   reflect a
Writer who is**
--under stress, overwhelmed, confused, experiencing varying mood shifts.

---Interesting Note:
--When you increase your concentration, your writing simultaneously becomes smaller.

--When you are tired of writing, you lose your ability to concentrate, and your writing
becomes larger.

How Does The Writer Respond To The Ups And Downs Of Reality?

The Baseline - The Line of Reality

---The Baseline is the line formed when writing Middle Zone Letters
--a c e i m n o r s u v w x

---The Baseline reflects a Writer's mood, disposition and ability to cope with the events of his/her Life.

---Placing a ruler under the Baseline will reveal the Baseline direction.

---A Level Baseline, parallel to the bottom of the page, reflects a
a Writer who is well-balanced, compliant, reliable, realistic,
emotionally stable, and effectively self-directed.

---A slightly, Bouncy Baseline reflects flexibility, versatility, a lively and happy
disposition.

---An Ascending, Rising Baseline reflects optimism, joy, hope, enthusiasm, excitement,
motivation, ambition, cheerfulness, healthy mental energy.

---A Descending, Downward Baseline reflects pessimism,
depression, discouragement, disillusionment, feeling of failure, fatigue, physical /
emotional problems.

---Moods constantly fluctuate. The Baseline reflects the changes.

RED ALERT!!!

---**An Extremely Irregular, Uneven Baseline reflects**
immaturity, moodiness, indecisiveness, anxiety, inconsistency.

A PERSONAL ENERGY PROFILE

---Discover what the Grapho-Indicators -- Spacing, Baseline, Slant, Pressure, Letter Size -- show and tell about your energy patterns.

---Use the PEP Checklist to record the findings in the Handwriting sample.

---Record the number of times the Grapho-Indicator is identified within the sample.

---Tally the findings on the appropriate line.

---Total the tally strokes.

---Place a check to the left of the line that indicates the highest total within each area.

---**A comprehensive, accurate Personal Energy Profile is based upon an assessment of <u>all Grapho-Indicators</u>.**
   Each Grapho-Indicator represents only part of the whole Individual.

---**Important Reminder:**

Each sample of Handwriting is a unique message revealing your energy pattern and emotional state <u>at the time</u> you place the graphic symbols on paper.

PERSONAL ENERGY PROFILE CHECKLIST

---Overall Organization - Clarity, Arrangement

Place a check on the appropriate line.

neat, orderly, balanced_____   disorganized_____

legible_____   illegible_____

---Spacing Between Lines

Your comfort level in relation to self and others.

	Tally	Total
_____Wide spacing	_____	_____
_____Narrow spacing	_____	_____
_____Inconsistent spacing	_____	_____

---Baseline

The direction of your mood and attitude.

Examine all Baselines in sample.

	Tally	Total
_____Up, ascending	_____	_____
_____Level	_____	_____
_____Down, descending	_____	_____
_____Erratic, uneven, wavering	_____	_____

---Slant

Reflects your temperament.

Examine a minimum of 30 upstrokes of letters b, h, k, I, from the beginning, middle, and end of sample.

	Tally	Total
____Right		
____Vertical		
____Left		
____Inconsistent, variable within any 10 consecutive letters		

---Pressure

Level of energy and vitality.

	Tally	Total
____Extremely dark, heavy		
____Moderately heavy		
____Light		
____ Variable, inconsistent		

---Letter Size

Your comfort level in relation to self and others
Measure Mid-Zone Letters.

	Tally	Total
_____Large		
_____ Moderate		
_____ Small		
_____ Variable		

Interpreting What The Grapho-Indicators Show And Tell

-- Overall Organization

    -- Illegibility and disorganization represents confusion, carelessness, impatience, inhibitions, nervousness, secrecy, non-conformity.

-- Spacing Between Lines

    -- **Wide Spacing** shows that the Writer isolates self from his/her environment- physically, socially, and emotionally.

    -- **Narrow Spacing** shows that the Writer has a need for contact with others.

    -- **Inconsistent, tangled Spacing** shows that the Writer is confused, frustrated, or overwhelmed.

-- Baseline - The kind of energy the Writer uses in dealing with the realities of Life.

    -- **Up, Ascending Baseline** shows that the Writer is optimistic, hopeful, joyful, ambitious, motivated.

    -- **Level Baseline** shows that the Writer is reliable, even-tempered, in control of his/her emotions, realistic, levelheaded.

    -- **Down, Descending Baseline** shows that the Writer is pessimistic, fatigued, discouraged, disappointed, unhappy, ill, depressed.

    -- **Erratic, Wavering Baseline** shows that the Writer is moody, indecisive, confused, temperamental, immature, anxious, frequently has "ups and downs".

-- Slant - The kind of energy the Writer uses in response to people, events, environment.

-- **Right Slant** shows that the Writer is extroverted, outgoing, friendly, affectionate, future oriented, seeks social interaction.

-- **Vertical Slant** shows that the Writer is level-headed, poised, disciplined, logical, independent, focuses on issues in the present time.

-- **Left Slant** shows that the Writer is introverted, uncommunicative, withdraws from social interaction, avoids emotional situations, seeks emotional security by retreating into the past.

-- **Variable Slant** shows that the Writer is conflicted, indecisive, unpredictable, insecure, unreliable.

-- Pressure - Level of energy, vitality, and determination

-- **Heavy Pressure** shows that the Writer is forceful, intense, aggressive.

-- **Moderately Heavy Pressure** shows that the Writer is energetic, determined, strong-willed, assertive.

-- **Light Pressure** shows that the Writer is sensitive, passive, lacks determination and vitality, may be physically weak.

-- **Variable, Inconsistent Pressure** shows that the Writer has an inconsistent energy level, erratic temperament, lacks self-discipline.

-- **Letter size**

    -- **Large Letter Size** shows that the Writer is extroverted, boastful, restless, needs to be noticed.

    -- **Moderate Letter Size** shows that the Writer is practical, realistic, adaptable, socially well-balanced.

    -- **Small Letter Size** shows that the Writer is introverted, modest, not too communicative, lacks self-confidence, has the ability to concentrate on facts. Poorly formed Small Letter Size shows that the Writer is not coping well with daily problems and routines.

    -- **Variable Letter Size** shows that the Writer is inconsistent, moody, indecisive, immature.

Food For Thought When Viewing A Child's Handwriting

--- Each Child has his/her own unique rate of Growth and Development.

--- Factors important to take into consideration
    -- Age, Emotional Maturity.
    -- Physical Health.
    -- Neuro-Muscular Development, Eye-Hand Coordination. Fine motor control is needed to make smooth round shapes. Girls develop fine muscle control earlier than boys.

--- Chemical sensitivities, allergies, drugs, alcohol, medications, illness, and fatigue can alter an individual's handwriting. Changes in Letter Size and Shape, Placement, and Pressure can be noted within 20 minutes after an allergic substance has entered the Body.

--- A young Child's lack of familiarity with the alphabet may cause distorted letter formation.

--- Slant in the early pre-teen and teen age years can be Vertical or slightly Left of center. A teenager may assume a more Right Slant when he/she feels more secure and confident in dealing with other people.

--- Some variations in Slant, Sizing, Spacing and Letter Formations naturally occur and are expected. No page of Handwriting contains Letter Formations that are uniform or identical in shape.
Too much variation and too much uniformity lacks rhythmical balance and harmony.

--- RED ALERT !!!

-- Grapho-Indicators appearing in a Child's writing, after the age of 9 show and tell Inner Conflict is in progress.

-- Blotches, scratches, heavy cross-outs, strike-overs, jumbled, altered letters, erasures, up and down Baselines show and tell that a Child is feeling extremely anxious, confused, and frustrated, fears making a mistake or doing something new.

-- Tangling of Letters show indecisiveness, confusion or visual difficulty.

-- Spurts of extremely Heavy Pressure and constant erasures show excessive worry, anger, indecisiveness, compulsiveness.

-- The secretive loop within the right side of the Circle Letters shows that a Child keeps his/her private thoughts and feelings locked up and resists conversations with authority figures. Fear and insecurity prevents a Child from freely expressing his/her thoughts and feelings. Any stroke within the circle letters "a", "o", "d," "g" interferes with open communication.

-- Closed "e and "1" listening loops show an Auditory System Shut-down--a resistance to listen.
Anger and Fear can cause an Auditory System Shut-down.

-- If a Child's Handwriting suddenly becomes extremely small, the Child is troubled, unhappy, and is retreating into a world of his/her own.

NOTE:

--- It Is Important To Keep An Ongoing Journal Of A Child's Handwriting
   Samples

      -- to monitor the fluctuating dynamics of a Child's Emotional Growth and Development.

      -- to focus in on a Child's Fears, Defense Strategies, and Thinking Patterns.

      -- to identify the existence of any Red Alert Signals.

      -- to determine if any Red Alert Signals are transitory or chronic in nature.

--- A combination of Red Alert Signals over an extended period of time shows and tells that a
   Child has a need to be heard and understood, and may require the attention and services
   of a Physical or Mental Health Professional.

TRAIT DETECTORS THAT SHOW AND TELL
EMOTIONAL AND INTELLECTUAL MATURITY
IN A CHILD'S HANDWRITING

A comprehensive, accurate evaluation of an Individual's Handwriting requires examination <u>of all</u> <u>Trait Detectors</u>.

- **Organization**
  - Rhythmic uniformity of letter formations.

  - Legibility--clear, uncluttered letter formations.

  - Consistent pattern of spacing for margins, lines, letters, and words.

- **Slant**
  - Consistent and rhythmical slant.

- **Pen Pressure**
  - Moderately heavy pen pressure.

  - Uniform pressure of t-bars.

- **Baseline**
  - Even or Ascending Baseline.

- **Style of Writing**
  - Simple strokes, well-formed letter formations.

A CHILD'S DEVELOPMENTAL WRITING SKILL SEQUENCE

Age   **Stage**

3 ½ - 4   -- Interest in letters in own name
                           -- Large single Capitals drawn at random
                           -- Circles drawn in clockwise direction
                           -- Some reversals in letter forms
                           -- Direction of strokes from right to left
                           -- Child has a narrow view of world and is Self- Centered.

4- 5   -- Undeveloped Neuro-Muscular Coordination
                           -- Large irregular printed letters
                           -- Some reversals in letter forms
                           -- Direction of strokes from left to right
                           -- Expansion of interest into environment from Self to others

6 - 7   -- Child learns to write the manuscript alphabet in
1st - 2nd grade   order to learn to read.
                           -- Large, irregular printed letters that tend to increase in size toward the
                              end of words.
                           -- Heavy pressure pattern the result of the intense Neuro-Muscular
                              effort required in making downstroke line formations and in
                              concentrating on form accuracy.
                           -- Ability to combine letters into simple words and sentences.

8-9   -- Child is ready to learn script letter formation
3rd - 4th grade   when he/she has learned to read.
                           -- With improved coordination of Neuro-Muscular movements, and
                              familiarity with letter shapes, letters become more uniform in size
                              and shape.
                           -- Slant will vary and ultimately conform to what is most comfortable
                              for the Individual.

Age	Stage
10- 11 5th - 6th grade	-- Pressure pattern developed. -- Round curves dominate. -- Uniqueness and individuality of writing style emerges. -- Child may alter speed, pressure, and letter shapes to meet his personal needs.
12- 15 7th - 9th grade	-- Variability in Slant, Pressure, Baseline, and Letter formations, reflect intense physiological and emotional bio-chemical changes, inner stress, confusion and emotional conflict.

WHAT TRAIT DETECTORS SHOW AND TELL IN A CHILD'S HANDWRITING

Age	Trait Detector	Shows and Tells
7-8	**Slant** -- Slight Left Trend	-- Self-centeredness
	-- Variable Slant	-- Writing technique not fully mastered -- Temporary emotional upset
	Pressure -- Heavy	-- Strong, active healthy child -- Difficulty in mastering pressure exerted by muscles
	Baseline -- Wavering, descending Baseline on unlined paper	-- Muscle control not fully developed -- Poor spatial judgment -- Unhappiness felt at moment of writing
	Letter Size -- Increased letter size at end of words and lines	-- Loss of concentration, fatigue
	Letter Shape -- Rounded "m" "n" formations	-- Letter formation is that of a Methodical Thinker
	-- Irregular, varied	-- Unfamiliar with letter shapes
	-- Altered Strokes	-- Attempt to perfect letters and deal with mistakes

Age	Trait Detector	Shows and Tells
9-11	**Slant**	
	-- Vertical	-- Appears calm and reserved
		-- Logical rather than emotional
	-- Moderately Right	-- Moderate temperament
		-- Responsible, considerate
		-- Balanced emotional expressiveness and logic
	-- Extreme Right	-- Impulsive, jumps to conclusions
		-- Overreacts, governed by emotions
		-- Inappropriate responses
	-- Left	-- Emotionally withdrawn
		-- Insecure, uncommunicative
	-- Extreme Left	-- Difficulty relating to others
		-- Fearful of future
	-- Variable	-- Insecure, inner conflicts
		-- Confusion, inconsistent, unpredictable, inappropriate responses

Age	Trait Detector	Shows and Tells
9-11	**Pressure**	
	-- Moderately Heavy	-- Healthy, energetic, will power
	-- Extremely Heavy	-- Anger, frustration, stress
		-- Harbors grudges and painful memories for long periods of time
	-- Extremely Light	-- Apathy, fatigue, passivity
		-- Indecisiveness, timidity
		-- Lacking will power and vitality
		-- Feelings of inadequacy
	-- Irregular, varied	-- Frustration, impatience
	Baseline	
	-- Ascending	-- Optimistic, hopeful, active
	-- Descending	-- Unhappiness, dissatisfaction, depression at time of writing
	-- Irregular, meandering	-- Anxiety, self-doubt, restlessness, moodiness

Age	Trait Detector	Shows and Tells
9-11	**Letter Size**	
	-- Large	-- Outgoing personality, people oriented
		-- Needs to be noticed and recognized
		-- Involved in activities
	-- Overly Large	-- Poor motor coordination
		-- Difficulty conforming to standards imposed by school or parents
	-- Small	-- Introverted personality
		-- Blocks out all distractions
		-- Uses concentration as an escape from having to deal with others
	-- Extremely Small	-- Extreme tension
		-- Shuts out people and environment to escape threatening situations in world of reality
	-- Small Capitals	-- Lacks confidence
	Letter Shapes	
	-- Pointed "m" "n"	-- Investigative Thinker
		-- Desires to learn new and different things
	-- Rounded "m" "n"	-- Logical, Methodical Thinker
	-- Poorly defined letter	-- Slow emotional, intellectual, or motor development
	-- Altered, overlapping Strokes	-- Fear, anxiety, insecurity, confusion
		-- Problem Thinker, difficulty in processing information

Age	Trait Detector	Shows and Tells
12-15	**Slant**	
	--Left	-- Emotional withdrawal
		-- Difficulty expressing emotions
		-- Experiencing unhappy, rebellious feelings
	-- Extreme Right	-- Impulsively overreacts to emotional stimuli
	-- Variable	-- Emotional conflicts, being pulled in different directions
	Pressure	
	-- Extremely Heavy	-- Frustration, stress, anger
		-- Keenly aware of senses of taste, smell, touch, sight, sounds, color
	-- Irregular, uneven	-- Emotional conflict
		-- Extra physical energy caused by hormonal changes
	Baseline	
	-- Wavy, uneven	-- Inner emotional conflict
	Letter Size	
	-- Variable	-- Fluctuating self-image

Age	Trait Detector	Shows and Tells
12-15	**Organization**	
	-- Lack of rhythm and balance	-- Withdrawn, hostility
	-- Blotches, heavy crossouts, strikeovers	-- Frustration, anger, stress
	-- Illegibility	-- Unwilling to openly communicate

A CHILD'S LEARNING STYLE FOR PROCESSING INFORMATION

---A Child's Learning Style does not determine I.Q

---A Child's Learning Style <u>does</u> reveal the reaction time in making
  decisions and the Primary Modality for Learning - Visual, Auditory,
  Kinesthetic.

---A Child's Learning Style is determined by the formation of the letters "m" " n"

THE VISUAL LEARNER - THE METHODICAL THINKER

(rounded tops)

--- is a slow, logical, thorough thinker.

--- uses verified reasoning at every step.

--- needs time to reach total understanding.

--- does not work well under pressure.

--- responds slowly to classroom questions and timed tests.

--- has difficulty in learning abstract subjects.

--- needs to re-read before comprehending.

--- follows directions carefully.

--- seems slow to grasp new ideas and concepts but when dealing with
      familiar material, thinks rapidly and accurately.

--- has difficulty in understanding <u>Auditory</u> instructions.

--- does well with visual clues: step by step written instructions,
      pictures, maps, charts

--- It is recommended that a Methodical Thinker not be asked for
      immediate oral feedback from what has just been explained.
      The Methodical Thinker needs time to think over the information,
      rearrange it and get comfortable with it before commenting.

THE LEFT BRAIN LEARNER - THE ANALYTIC THINKER
(baseline "v"'s)

--- analyzes information carefully before coming to a
    conclusion.
--- asks questions, seeks answers, is eager to learn.
--- is impatient to get things done his own way and according to his own
    rules.
--- deals with an abundance of information without confusion.
--- is a good problem solver.

--- The Analytic Thinker must be challenged with problems, riddles and
    puzzles to solve.

AUDITORY LEARNER – INVESTIGATIVE THINKER (inverted "v"'s)

--- is curious, always inquiring, wants to know "why" to everything.
--- grasps information without studying too hard.
--- adjusts to a variety of situations quickly.
--- has an agile mind.
--- becomes restless with slow repeated methodical instructions or
    visual cues.
--- has practical knowledge of many things.
--- seeks new challenges.
--- is good at almost anything he wants to do.
--- resents the efforts of others to influence his decisions.

--- The Investigative Thinker should be given opportunity to structure
    his curiosity into productive projects.

THE KINESTHETIC LEARNER - THE COMPREHENSIVE THINKER

(needle-pointed)

--- has keen comprehension.

--- grasps concepts, ideas, and situations almost instantly.

--- jumps to conclusions without giving serious thought to the total

--- adapts easily to new circumstances.

--- is insightful and perceptive.

--- makes decisions without having to mull it over.

--- is intelligent, a good conversationalist, a good student.

--- becomes restless and bored with slow methodical instructions.

--- is a mentally and physically active person.

--- It is essential to keep the Comprehensive Thinker busy and challenged
    in a productive manner.

CHILDHOOD FEARS

--- A Child responds with Fear to what he/she feels and believes to be unsafe events, actions, or experiences.

--- It is the responsibility of Primary Caregivers and Teachers to recognize
  -- the existence of Fear and Anxiety in a Child.
  -- the Defense Strategies that a Child uses to deal with feelings of Fear and Anxiety.
  -- the negative messages and experiences that generate Fear and Anxiety.
  -- the supportive measures needed to help a Child appropriately deal with his/her Fears.
  -- the Grapho-Indicators that show and tell the feelings a Child experiences, but is unable to verbally express.

--- **IMPORTANT TO NOTE:**

  -- A Child's Fears are not to be lightly dismissed or ignored.

  -- A Child's Fears are not to be judged to be true or false, good or bad, right or wrong.

  -- Unresolved Childhood Fears affect an Individual's ability to effectively function in the later years.

THE ORIGIN OF CHILDHOOD FEARS

--- Physical Safety and Emotional Security are basic needs for every Human Being.

--- A child feels Fear when his/her physical or emotional safety is threatened.

--- Negative messages, traumatic experiences, and painful actions threaten a Child's Sense of Security and cause a Child to feel Fear.

--- Fear is Emotional Insecurity.

--- Fear generates Anxiety and Anger --Stress and Tension.

--- Fear takes root during the early Childhood Years.

--- Fear interferes with a Child's ability to concentrate.

--- Fear stunts a Child's positive Physical and Emotional Growth.

--- Fear interferes with a Child's ability to develop and maintain healthy relationships.

--- Fear is at the root of behavioral and personality problems.

-- Child feels inadequate, unaccepted, unworthy, inferior to others,
uncomfortable in unfamiliar surroundings.

-- Child lacks Self-Confidence and Self Esteem.

-- Child has difficulty functioning effectively, fears making
mistakes, and anticipates receiving hurtful criticisms.

-- Negative Experiences
-- A Child is repeatedly ridiculed, humiliated, embarrassed, teased, insulted by Primary
Caregivers, Peers, or Adults.

-- Supportive Measures Needed
-- encouragement, compliments, recognition for his/her unique strengths and abilities.

-- Grapho-Indicators that show and tell the Fear of Ridicule

-- m's with a higher last hump

-- double letters ee, 11, tt, ff - in which the 2nd letter is taller than the first

-- the higher the last hump, the taller the 2nd letter, the stronger the Fear.

Fear of Disapproval -- Sensitivity to Criticism

-- Child feels rejected, inadequate, discouraged.

-- Child has low Self Esteem.

-- **Negative Experiences**
  -- Focus is on what Child cannot do.
  -- Child is repeatedly subjected to hurtful criticisms, complaints, accusations, fault finding, unfavorable comparisons to others.

- - **Supportive Measures Needed**
  -- **CPR**
    -- consistent, constructive, corrective positive reinforcement.
      -- compliments, praise, respect, reassurance, recognition for every small step on the road to achievement.

    -- Focus on what Child can do -- accentuating Child's positive strengths, skills, and abilities.

-- **Grapho-Indicators that show and tell the Fear of Disapproval**

-- enlarged d loop - sensitivity to criticism about personal appearance

d

-- enlarged t loop - sensitivity to criticism about work performance or accomplishments

t

-- the greater the size of the loop, the greater the intensity of Fear.

Fear of Failure -- Fear of the Future, Fear of Change

-- Child feels incompetent, unimportant, inferior to others.

-- Child is unwilling to take risks, because he/she expects to fail.

-- Child lacks will power, purpose, direction, self-confidence

-- **Negative Experiences**
    -- Primary Caregivers and/or teachers use pressure to impose unrealistic
       expectations upon a Child who is not ready to achieve such goals.

-- **Supportive Measures Needed**
    -- encouragement and support to achieve those goals that are realistically
       adjusted in accordance with his/her abilities.

-- **Grapho-Indicator that shows and tells the Fear of Failure**

-- low t-bar crossing on t-stem _____ t _____

Fear of Not Being Loved -- Jealousy

-- Child feels threatened and resents the need to share Parental love and attention.

-- Child fears that someone will take his/her place and regards Everyone as a rival.

-- Child feels unloved, unappreciated, neglected, abandoned, rejected.

-- **Painful Experience**
  -- The arrival of a new sibling and the Fear of losing Parental love.

-- **Supportive Measures Needed**
  -- the nurturing a's -- acceptance, acknowledgment, affection, appreciation, approval, attention.
  -- frequent physical and verbal reassurances -- plenty of daily hugs, kisses, smiles, praise.

-- **Grapho-Indicator that shows and tells the presence of Jealousy**

  -- tight small loops at beginning of Capital Letters W N M T

Repression -- Fear of Self – Expression -- Blocked Communication

-- Child has difficulty recognizing and expressing his/her true feelings.

-- Child becomes tense and uptight.

-- Child has problems coping with Worries and Fears.

-- Child's ability to interact with other Children and Adults is impaired.

-- **Negative Experience**
  -- Child is taught that it is not okay to cry or freely express his/her angry, hurt feelings.

-- **Supportive Measures Needed**
  -- reassurances that it is okay to appropriately express hurt and angry feelings and is given opportunities to do so.

-- **Grapho-Indicators that show and tell the presence of Repression**
  -- crowded, tight retraced writing
  -- cramped narrow letters that are difficult to read
  -- no space between m n h humps

IMPORTANT TO NOTE:
-- Human Beings have a strong need to express their feelings in order to relieve Inner Stress and Tension.

-- If hurt feelings are not appropriately expressed, they become repressed--buried, denied, hidden, ignored, unresolved

-- Repressed Feelings produce a toxic build-up of Inner Tension and Stress-- Fear, Anger, Anxiety--and contribute to stress related physical disorders that seriously affect personality and behavior.

Defense Strategies -- Methods of Dealing with Real or Imagined Fears

--- There are three **Defense Trait Categories**.

-- Resistance Traits
-- Resisting the presence of Fear by reacting with hostility.
-- Evidence of too many Resistance Traits in one Handwriting Sample, reveals a troubled Child with behavioral problems.

-- Escape Traits
-- Seeking to emotionally escape the reality of Fear.
-- Evidence of too many Escape Traits in one Handwriting Sample reveals a Child with personality problems who is not actively participating in real life.

-- Adjustment Traits
-- Using socially acceptable strategies that effectively confront, deal, and adjust to the ever present Fears, problems, and realities of Life.
-- Evidence of Adjustment Traits in a Handwriting Sample reveals an Individual's Emotional Maturity.

--- The Resistance and Escape Traits are reactions to Fear and insecurity suffered from past painful experiences. Both categories of Defense Strategies reflect an Individual's Emotional Immaturity.

Resistance Traits -- Anti-Social, Hostility Traits

- **Defiance**
  - Anger and rebellion toward authority figures.
  - Indicates the Fear of being dominated, humiliated, or controlled by others.

  - Grapho-Indicator
    - oversized buckle of letter "k"

- **Domineering**
  - Tendency to be overbearing, demanding, manipulative.
  - Indicates insecurity - attempting to focus upon another Individual's vulnerabilities in order to distract from one's own inadequacies.
    - Tendency begins in Childhood where an excessively controlling, demanding, parentally dominated environment exists.

  - **Grapho-Indicator**
    - pointed t-bar, slanting downward

--**Irritability**
  - Impatience with self, others, or circumstances.
  - Indicates Fear and Frustration triggered by Inner Tension.

  - **Grapho-Indicator**
    - distorted dots - irregular short dashes over "i's " and "j'

  -- t-bar to the right of t-stem – not touching the stem

--Resentment
  -- Built up inner Anger and Annoyance
  -- Indicates harboring of grudges about unforgiven past injustices, guarded, chip-on-the-
      shoulder attitude.

  -- **Grapho-Indicator**
      -- straight , inflexible, initial stroke that begins at or below
        the Baseline

-- **Sarcasm**
  -- A cutting, verbal attack to express contempt for someone.
  -- The tongue is used as a sharp weapon to launch the verbal attack.
  -- Indicates Individual feels threatened.

  -- **Grapho-Indicator**
    -- t-bar with needle-pointed ending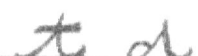

-- **Stubbornness**
  -- Firm convictions, refusal to yield or change opinions.
  -- Indicates that Individual feels yielding is a sign of weakness.

  -- **Grapho-Indicator**
    -- inverted v formation of "t" and "d" stem

--- Escape Traits -- Withdrawal Strategies

-- Clannishness
- -- Selectively restricting social contact.
- -- Indicates Fear, insecurity and mistrust of those who are different from Self.

-- Grapho-Indicator

- -- small, tight lower loop below the Baseline

-- Concentration
- -- Using the powers of concentration to shut out the world of Reality.
- -- Blocking out all unwanted ideas, thoughts, and sounds.
- -- Living in a narrow world of self thoughts.
- -- Indicates that Individual has extreme difficulty in dealing with Emotions.

-- Grapho-Indicator
- -- very small writing - Middle Zone Letters less than 1/16

- - Daydreaming
- -- Escaping from unhappy reality by building a fantasy world.

-- Grapho-Indicator
- -- light, weak t-bar floating above stem

--Irresponsibility
- -- Seeking to physically and emotionally escape from unwanted pressure by withdrawing and not communicating with anyone involved in the problem situation.
- -- Indicates weak Will Power and a lack of Confidence in Self and in one's abilities.

-- Grapho-Indicator
- -- shallow cup shaped t-bars

--Procrastination
   -- Postponing a disliked activity.
   -- Reluctance to face the Present and Future.
   -- Indicates Insecurity, Fear of Failure, Fear of Criticism, Fear of Challenge - a reaction to the pressure of high, demanding expectations.

   - - **Grapho-Indicator**
      -- t-bars to the left of t-stem
         indicate a delay in dealing with anything related to goals
         or plans for the Future.

      -- i-dots and j-dots to the left of the stems
         indicate a delay in dealing with details of Life.

- - **Secrecy**
   -- Preventing effective communication by withholding information or facts from others.
   -- Indicates difficulty with honesty and directness, insecurity, guilt, and Fear of Rejection.

   -- **Grapho-Indicator**
      -- final loop placed in right side of circle letters "a" "o"

- - **Self-deceit**
   -- Escaping the unpleasantness of Reality by not seeing things as they are but as Individual wishes them to be.
   -- Refusing to directly confront facts, issues, problems.
   -- Jumping to conclusions based upon faulty assumptions and incomplete information.
   -- Using excuses to rationalize and justify motives and actions.
   -- Indicates blocking of past, painful early life experiences, and ineffective communication with Self.

   -- **Grapho-Indicator**
      -- initial left loop on inside of circle letters "a" and "o"

--- Adjustment Traits -- Coping Strategies

--Decisiveness
-- Making firm decisions after considering all alternatives.
-- Indicates Courage.

-- **Grapho-Indicator**
   -- firm stroke endings

--Determination
-- Willingness to exert the time and energy needed to achieve goals and complete
   projects.
-- **Grapho-Indicator**
   -- straight stroke descending below the Baseline, twice the size of Middle Zone
      Letters.

-- Dignity / Pride
--   Desiring to conform to
        a socially acceptable code of behavior.
   -- Doing one's best at all times.
   -- Achieving what one sets out to do.
-      **Grapho-Indicator**
      -- retraced t-stem - pride about work

      -- retraced d-stem - pride about appearance

-- Diplomacy
   -- Exhibiting tact and consideration toward others.

   -- **Grapho-Indicator**
      -- last stroke of "m" lower than the first

-- **Loyalty/ Attention to details**
   -- Being faithful to one's ideals.
   -- Paying attention to details.

   -- **Grapho-Indicator**
      -- dots close to stems of "i's" and j's"

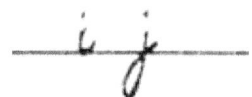

--Reticence
   -- Choosing to speak honestly and openly when there is something important to be said.
   -- Indicates a tactful, responsible, attentive listener.

   -- **Grapho-Indicator**
      -- uncluttered circle letters "a" "o" closed at the top

-- **Will Power**
   -- Willing to set realistic goals.
   -- Trusting in one's ability to succeed.
   -- Indicates Self-Confidence and high Self-Esteem.

   -- **Grapho-Indicator**
      -- strong, balanced t-bar, placed close to the top of the t-stem

Children Need US TO Overcome Childhood Fears

--Understanding, Unconditional Love

--Security, a Sense of Success

--- **Riddle:**

1) What is a 4 letter word that stands for nurturing?

2) What is a 4 letter word that stands for deprivation?

--- Four letter word messages that are worthy of constant repetition.

-- Free your Life from Fear, Hurt, Pain.

-- Fill your Life with Love plus Hope.

Answers to Riddle

1) Love
2) Fear

THE MANY SIDES AND SIGNS OF DEPRESSION

--- **Depression**
  -- A reaction to an upsetting event or loss.
  -- An Individual's inability to accept what is.
  -- An Individual's inability to appropriately express painful feelings.
  -- Can affect any Individual regardless of age, gender, or socio-economic level.
  -- Can have varying degrees of intensity and duration.
    -- mild, moderate, severe, transitory, persistent

--- **A Depressed Person**
  -- experiences the painful feelings of Low Self-Esteem--hopelessness, helplessness, worthlessness, self-directed hostility.
  -- expresses emotional pain in self-destructive, risk taking, abusive behaviors.

  --- **Causes**
    -- Change in family structure .divorce, death, illness.
    -- Loss of someone or something that has been loved.
    -- Deprivation of love in Childhood.
    -- Chemical changes within the Body.

--- **Childhood and Teenager Depression**
    -- retards a child's Positive Emotional Growth and Development.
    -- negatively affects a Child's personal and social relationships.
    -- interferes with a Child's ability to function effectively.

--- Masked Depression in School Age Children

-- Behavioral Clues
- -- Child appears to be moody, indifferent, listless, rebellious, aggressive, defiant.
- -- Child has
  - -- difficulty concentrating.
  - -- poor sleeping and eating habits.
  - -- unexplained physical symptoms of headaches, stomach aches, vague aches, and pains.
  - -- loss of interest in activities previously enjoyed.

-- Causes
- -- Family Conflicts and Tension.
- -- Parental Neglect or Abuse--physical, verbal, emotional, or sexual.
- -- Love Deprivation.
- -- Severe loss or separation from a meaningful relationship with persons or pets . divorce, death.
- -- Chronic Illness.
- -- Peer Rejection.
- -- Environmental changes in home, school.

--- Masked Depression in Teenagers

-- Behavioral Clues
- -- Outwardly acts tough, boisterous, rebellious, irrational, impulsive, defiant, hyperactive.
- -- Acts indifferent to surroundings, environment, people, events.
- -- A short attention span and inability to concentrate.
- -- Disturbed sleep patterns.
- -- Accident prone.
- -- Pre-occupation with thoughts of death.
- -- Engages in self-destructive, risk taking, abusive behavior.
  - -- alcohol, drugs --depressants that increase depression.
  - -- promiscuity -- increase in teen age pregnancies.
  - -- smoking.
  - -- eating disorders.
  - -- obsessive compulsions.
  - -- reckless driving.

-- Self-destructive behavior reflects underlying Feelings of Self -Hate and Self-Doubt.

--- Childhood Depression can lead to Suicide.

-- Suicide is
   -- a cry for help to be noticed.
   -- an attempt to end the pain of Depression.
   -- a self-destructive message that may be verbal or written.

-- Causes
   -- A sudden loss of an important relationship.
   -- Fear of Rejection.
   -- Fear of Failure--inability to live up to parent's unrealistic expectations.
   -- Self- Hate, Self-Doubt, Low Self-Esteem.

--- Behavioral Clues
   -- Inability to cope with the routine tasks of daily living.
   -- Withdrawal from family, friends, and activities.
   -- Giving away favorite possessions.
   -- Increased use of drugs and /or alcohol.
   -- Inability to concentrate, confused irrational thinking.
   -- Academic failure.
   -- Loss of appetite.
   -- Sleep disturbances.
   -- Not goal oriented.

**--- All Suicide Threats - expressed verbally or in writing-
     must be taken seriously.**
   -- Suicide Threats are not to be denied, belittled or minimized.
   -- If you fear that someone is suicidal, never leave that person alone.
   -- Seek immediate professional help. Contact a Crisis Center.

--- <u>Parents and Teachers must learn to recognize the Emotional, Behavioral, and Graphic signs of Depression and Suicide.</u>

--- <u>Parents and Teachers must frequently review a Childs handwriting sample to note any significant negative changes that may reflect the presence of Depression.</u>

--- **Grapho-Indicators can show and tell Depression or Suicidal Intent.**
   -- <u>**A combination of Indicators must be present to have an accurate assessment of Depression**</u>.
   -- Extremes and inconsistencies in Slant, Pressure, Letter Size.
   -- Illegible, tangled script.
   -- Descending, erratic Baseline--words or word endings that droop below the Baseline.
   -- Weak, poorly formed t-bars.
   -- Distorted letter formations, patched letters.

--- **Note:**
   -- Suicidal people usually kill themselves on impulse.
   -- A Suicidal Baseline may involve only a few lines or words on a page of writing.
   -- A descent may suddenly appear in the last word or words, or last letters of a word at the end of a line at the right margin.
   -- Studies have indicated that people who had successfully committed Suicide, tended to write short Suicide notes.
   -- Those who were unsuccessful in their Suicide attempts, wrote long notes and managed to be saved in time.

RECOGNIZING THE SIGNS OF ANGER

--- **Anger**
  -- A natural emotion - here to stay, never goes away, can be experienced by any Individual -- regardless of age, gender, or socio-economic level -- any time, any place.
  -- Comes in many forms, shapes, sizes, intensities - frustration, hostility, irritability, impatience, jealousy, hate, fury, greed, moodiness, procrastination, resentment, rage.
  -- A reaction to painful traumatic experiences of abandonment, abuse - verbal, emotional, physical, or sexual, betrayal, deprivation, neglect, or rejection.
  -- Necessary to be identified, released, defused, and appropriately expressed.
  -- If ignored or denied, will fester and become toxic Repressed Anger.

--- **Why Repressed Anger is hazardous to your Emotional and Physical Well-Being.**
  -- Destroys Self-Esteem.
  -- Adversely affects every relationship, by interfering with a person's ability to trust and relate well with others.
  -- Keeps an Individual stuck in the period of time when the painful experience occurred, perpetuating pain and tension, retarding Emotional Growth.
  -- Prevents an Individual from achieving a satisfactory resolution to a problem.
  -- Increase in intensity to explosive levels of Rage and Violence against One's Self and Others.

--- **Repressed Anger in School Age Children**
  -- **Behavioral Clues**
      -- Appears boisterous, rebellious defiant.
      -- Engages in Self-Destructive, Addictive, Abusive Behavior.
          -- alcohol, drugs, smoking
          -- eating disorders
      -- Violates the safety of Others.
      -- Disrespects the rights of Others.
      -- Annoys, humiliates, insults, ridicules, teases, threatens Others.

Self Destructive Behavior reflects underlying Feelings of SELF HATE and SELF DOUBT.

"t-bars" and "i-dots" SHOW AND TELL FEELINGS OF ANGER

--- Count the number of "t-bars" in any Handwriting Sample.
   TOTAL_____

--- Tally and total the number of "t-bars"
   to the left of the "t-stem" _____ Total _____

   to the right of the "t-stem" _____ Total _____

   that are long, strong, balanced, and placed close to the top of the "t-stem"
   _____ Total _____

--- What the "t-bars" show and tell
   -- The number of "t-bars" to the left of the "t-stem", in comparison to the total number of "t-bars", shows and tells the degree of Procrastination and Frustration a Writer experienced at the time of writing.

   -- The number of "t-bars" to the right of the "t-stem", in comparison to the total number of "t-bars", shows and tells how much Anger a Writer experienced at the time of writing.

   -- The number of long, strong "t-bars", in comparison to the total number of "t-bars", shows and tells the level of Confidence a Writer experienced at the time of writing.

--- Count the number of "i" and "j" dots in a Handwriting Sample.
   Total _____

--- Tally and Total the number of "i" and "j" dots that are slashes.
   _____ Total _____

--- Tally and Total the number of "i" and "j" dots that are dots placed close to the stem
   _____ Total _____

--- What the "i" and "j" dots show and tell

   -- The number of dot slashes, in comparison to the total number of i-dots, shows and tells the degree of Irritability and Impatience a Writer experienced at the time of writing.

   -- The number of i-dots placed close to the stem, in comparison to the total number of i-dots, shows and tells how Accurate, and Observant a Writer was at the time of writing.

POSITIVELY ENERGIZED ESTEEM TEAM LETTER FORMATIONS

It Does Matter How You Cross Your "t's" And Dot Your "i's".

-- You are only a line away from setting realistic Goals, having
Self-Confidence and strong Willpower.
-- t-bars that are long, strong, balanced and placed close to the top of the t-stem show and
tell that the writer has Self-Confidence, High Self Esteem, sets realistic,
achievable Goals, and has the power to overcome everyday obstacles.

--- You are only a dot away from being observant, attentive, and improving your memory.

--- Well-rounded "e" and "l" loops, and well-rounded, clear
circle letters "a" "o", can sharpen your Learning,
Listening, and Communicating Skills.

--- Even, or descending "m" and " n" humps can make you feel Socially
Comfortable and Poised.

--- Learning to write the Esteem Team Letter Formations can give you
POSITIVE ENERGY POWER (PEP).

THE WRITE WAY TO LEARN THE ESTEEM TEAM LETTER FORMATIONS

--- Use 8 1/2 x 11 size unlined paper.

--- Concentrate on one Letter Formation at a time.

--- The Trait Detector tells you the positive shape of the Team Letter.

--- Practice writing the Key Word and Sentences for 20/30 minutes a
   day for 30 consecutive days. It takes a minimum of 30 days to
   program a new habit into your Memory Data Bank.
   Verbalizing the sentences as you write, speeds the learning process.

--- Check for consistency and accuracy of the new Letter Formation.

--- Repeat the practice for another 30 days, if you find inconsistencies in
   the Letter Formation. Inconsistency means the habit has not been
   completely programmed into your Memory Data Bank.

--- Monitor your Esteem Team Letter Formations after all written entries.
   Your Esteem Team shows and tells what shape you are in.

--- Repeat the programming process for each Letter change.

Note:

--- Your Brain is designed to program one habit change at a time.

--- Your Brain is not designed to make sudden instant changes.

--- Attempting to change more than one Trait Stroke at the same time
   leads to a state of Confusion.

--- The length of time to learn a new habit varies for each Person. For
   some it may be a month. For some it may be several months.

--- Positive habits require constant reinforcement to remain a part of
   your Positive Thinking Pattern.

--- **Key Words For Successful Reprogramming:**
   Commitment—Consistency -- Patience -- Practice -- Repetition

--- **IMPORTANT REMINDER: ONE LETTER CHANGE AT A TIME!!!**

TIME TO USE THE TEAM OF LETTER FORMATIONS
THAT
LEAD TO A GOOD SELF-IMAGE AND JOY

Letters "t" "e" "l" "i" "j" "a" "o" "m"

A good Self-Image provides the Positively Energized Power (PEP) needed to successfully cope with the realities of Life.

TIME TO TAKE ON THE TRIUMPHANT "t's" THAT TOUT SELF-ESTEEM

Personality Trait	Trait Detector
-- Self-confidence -- Pride in achievement	-- Height of t-stem: twice the size of middle-zone letters-a, e, i, o, u
-- Strong will power	-- Strong, long straight t-bar, evenly crossed on t-stem
-- Ambition -- Ability to set and achieve realistic, practical goals	-- t-bar placed close to the top of t-stem
-- Enthusiasm	-- Long, straight t-bar, slanted upward

Key Words
-- triumph
-- strength
-- trust
-- time

Key Statements
-- I take the time to set realistic goals.
-- I take the time to appreciate my achievements.
-- I take the time to do my best.
-- I trust in my strength and ability to triumph.
-- I feel great about me.
-- I have strong faith and belief in myself.

Note:
-- The length, pressure, placement, and shape of the t-bar shows and tells the force behind the Will Power.
-- Will Power supplies the drive necessary to overcome all obstacles.
-- WILL POWER TRANSLATES WISHES INTO ACTION.

TIME FOR CIRCLE LETTERS AND LISTENING LOOPS TO FORM THE LINES FOR HONEST OPEN COMMUNICATION
"a's" "o's" "e's" "l's"

Personality Trait	Trait Detector
-- Broadmindedness	-- Well-rounded circle letters
-- Honesty, Frankness	-- Clear, uncluttered circle letters
-- Attentive Listener	-- Well-rounded "1" loops
-- Open attitude to new ideas	-- Letter height, twice the size of
-- Accepting of information from others	middle zone letters a, e, i, o, u
-- Openmindedness	-- Well-rounded "e" loops
-- Willingness to learn and accept new ideas	
-- Good listener	
-- Good memory--remembers what is heard	

Key Words

- -- respect
- -- learn
- -- listen
- -- look
- -- observe
- -- open, honest communication

Key Statements

    -- I respect myself and others.

    -- I can learn a great deal when I listen to new ideas.

    -- I feel good when I am happy.

    -- I am learning to enjoy each day.

    -- I listen with respect to the opinions of others, even though I may not agree with their views.

    -- I am able to be a good listener.

    -- I thoughtfully evaluate all aspects of an issue.

    -- I communicate when I openly express my inner feelings.

    -- I am an open, honest communicator.

TIME FOR "i" AND "j" DOTS TO BE ATTENTIVELY LOYAL TO THEIR STEMS

Personality Trait

-- Dependable, reliable
-- Loyal, faithful to one's ideals
-- Attentive to detailed work
     requiring eye-hand coordination
-- Good memory

Trait Detector

-- Dots placed close to "i" and "j" stems

Key Words

-- attention
-- details
-- ideals
-- interest

-- just
-- joy
-- joint

Key Statements

-- It is in my best interests to pay attention to what I do.

-- I believe it is important to enjoy each day.

-- When I pay attention to details, I can remember what it is I see.

-- I join in activities just for the joy of it.

-- Every joint in my body feels my joy.

-- Each day, I am learning that the number of pleasures to enjoy in life are just infinite.

TIME TO MONITOR THE "m's" FOR MANY MOMENTS
OF EMOTIONAL EASE AND DIPLOMACY

Personality Trait	Trait Detector
-- Tact	-- Descending height of "m" humps
-- Diplomacy	
-- Confidence	
-- Consideration toward others	

Key Words

   -- diplomacy

   -- maximum

   -- momentum

Key Statements

   -- I make the most of my time.

   -- I do not make mountains out of molehills.

   -- I am able to overcome major obstacles when I make up my mind to do so.

   -- I create miles of smiles for myself when I think of the many pleasant memories
         stored in my mind.

   -- Confidence in myself gives me momentum to achieve.

   -- I maximize the positive and minimize the negative.

   -- I feel good about myself

ESTEEM TEAM LETTER SHAPE CHECK LIST

Whenever you do any writing, check the shape of your Esteem Team Letters.

-- For Confidence and Will Power
> "t- bars" -- long, strong, evenly balanced, crossed close to the top
> of the "t" stem

-- For Honest, Open Communication
> "a" " o" -- clean uncluttered circles

-- For Learning and Listening
> "e" "l" -- well—rounded loops

-- For Accuracy, Improved Memory and Observational Skills
> "i" "j" -- dots placed close to the stem

-- To Feel Socially Comfortable
> "m" "n" -- descending or even height of humps

Your Esteem Team Positively Empowers You To Be A Winner !!!

FOOD FOR THOUGHT

FROM THE POINT OF VIEW OF A GUIDANCE COUNSELOR AND HANDWRITING ANALYST

HANDWRITING IS REALLY BRAINWRITING!!!
-- *Brain Impulses direct all Activity and Movements.*
-- *Learning to write involves the entire Neuro-Muscular System.*
-- *The Neuro-Muscular Skill of Handwriting becomes a habit that is stored in the Brain's Memory Data Bank.*
-- *When it is time for Written Communication, the Brain accesses the Writing Skill Program from the Memory Data Bank and sends Neuro-Muscular Impulses to the Hand.*
-- *The Hand moves the pen to record the Feelings, Thoughts, and Ideas that the Brain wishes to express.*
-- *The Hand is the Neuro-Muscular Connection between the Brain and the paper.*

FACTORS THAT CONTRIBUTE TO A NEGATIVE LEARNING EXPERIENCE IN HANDWRITING
-- *CORRECTING OR CRITICISING A WRITER'S SLANT OR LETTER SIZE*
  -- *Interferes with an Individual's unique Personality Traits.*
  -- *Stifles Individuality, Creativity, Originality.*
  -- *Causes Fear, Anxiety, Inhibition, Insecurity, <u>LOW SELF ESTEEM.</u>*

-- *UNNECESSARY STROKES -- Initial Strokes, Flourishes, Embellishments*
  -- *Reduce handwriting speed, rhythm, and legibility.*
  -- *Involve intricate, labored, muscle movements.*
  -- *Interrupt the flow of thoughts.*
  -- *Cause Frustration, Confusion, Tension.*

Low Self Esteem, originating in Childhood, can contribute to the Problems and Difficulties an Individual experiences throughout his/her Life.

Positive Learning Experiences nurture a Child's Healthy, Emotional Growth and Personality Development.

SIMPLE SCRIPT -- A POSITIVE PRIMARY LEARNING EXPERIENCE

-- *Easy to learn, write, and read.*

-- *Simplifies a complex learning skill by using simple uncluttered letter formations to record thoughts, ideas, and feelings.*

-- *Simplifies the transition from Printing to Script by adding a curved stroke to the endings of many familiar Manuscript Letters.*

-- *Accommodates those Children whose Neuromuscular Skills are underdeveloped.*

-- *Permits the Writer's time, energy, and effort to focus on thought content.*

-- *Encourages positive emotional expression and open communication.*

-- *Achieves legibility, speed, and rhythm in handwriting.*

--- *Focuses in on the Letter Shapes that boost a Writer's Self Esteem.*
  -- *Large, simple well-formed Capital Letters*
  -- *High, firmly placed "t-bars"*
  -- *Clear, rounded "a's" and "o's"*
  -- *Moderately rounded "e" and "l" loops*

SIMPLE SCRIPT ALPHA - FACTS

CAPITAL LETTERS

-- *Height for all Capital Letters*
   2 - 2 1/2 times the size of middle zone letters a, e, i, o, u

Simple Script Capital Letters do not connect to the next letter and are the same as Manuscript Capital Letters.

A B C D E F G H I J K L M N O P Q R S T

U V W X Y Z

SIMPLE SCRIPT ALPHA- FACTS

LOWER CASE LETTERS

--- *Letters that are similar to their Upper Case Letters*

c o p s v w x z

--- *Letters that end with a curved stroke*

a d h i k m n t u

TopLine

Mid-Line

BaseLine   *b l e r*

--- **9** *New Letter Shapes*

-- *Tall letters " b" and "1"*

    -- *Initial upward curve starts at the Base Line, ends close to the Top Line. Straight downward stroke to the Base Line. End with a curve. Aim for moderate size loops.*

    -- *Letter " b" has a short curve ending at the Mid-Line.*

-- *Short letters "e" and r*

    -- *Letter "e"*

        Initial upward curve starts at the Base Line, ends at the Mid-Line. Short straight downstroke to the Base Line. End with a curve. Aim for moderate size loop.

    -- *Letter "r"*

        Begin initial upward curve at the Base Line. Extend curve to the Mid-Line. Short slanted horizontal line, followed by a straight line to the Base Line. End with a curve.

TopLine

Mid-Line

BaseLine

q j q y f

---Long Letters "g" "j" "q" "y" "f"

-- *Letters "g" "j" "q" "y"*

Extend the curved loop up to the Base Line.

-- *Letter "f"*

Start curve at the Base Line. End curve close to the Top Line. Extend straight downstroke to 1/2 space below the Base Line. Upward curve stroke to the Base Line. End with a curve.

Upper and lower loops are on the right side of the vertical line.

---Note:

-- *Downstrokes are straight, firm lines.*

-- *"i" and " j" dots are placed close to their stems.*

-- *Letters " a",, "o", " d", " g", "q", have clear, uncluttered circles.*

-- *Well-rounded loops for Letters " e" and " 1".*

-- *Even or descending "m" humps.*

-- *t-bar is a long, strong, evenly balanced horizontal line moving forward from left to right and placed close to the top of the t-stem.*

POSITIVE THOUGHTS PROVIDE POSITIVE ENERGY POWER !!!

YOU ARE WHAT YOU BEL1EVE !!!

--- *Start a Personal Daily Journal.*

--- *Select 3 POSITIVE THOUGHTS at a time.*

--- *Write the 3 thoughts, 3 times each, for one week.*

--- *Every week, choose another 3 thoughts to add to your entry.*

--- *Continue to increase the number of thoughts so that the writing exercise lasts for 20/ 30 minutes.*

--- *Journal entries written shortly before going to bed, can help you to have a good night's sleep.*

P0SITIVE THOUGHTS TO WRITE, TO READ, TO BELIEVE

-- *I am unique.*

-- *I am an important person.*

-- *I am a winner.*

-- *I am a good listener.*

-- *I am proud of myself.*

-- *I aim to be the best that I can be.*

-- *I appreciate all the good things I can do.*

-- *I believe that I am a success.*

-- *I believe that I can do anything that I make up my mind to do.*

-- *I have a good attitude.*

-- *I have the power to solve my problems.*

-- *I have faith in my ability to achieve.*

-- *I have self control.*

-- *I have will power.*

-- *I like who I am.*

-- *I think good thoughts*

-- *I value myself.*

FEELINGS -- YOUR SOURCE OF EMOTIONAL ENERGY

--- Feelings influence what you Think.
- -- What you Think influences what you Believe.
- -- What you Believe influences how you Act.
- -- How you Act influences your Relationships with others.

--- Only one Feeling can be expressed at any one time.
- -- When you feel Love, you do not feel Anger.
- -- When you feel Happy, you do not feel Sad.
- -- When you feel Secure, you do not feel Fear.
- -- When you smile, you do not frown.
- -- When you hug, you do not fight.
- -- When you laugh, you do not cry.
- -- When you compliment, you do not criticize.

--- When you feel Comfortable, you like the way you feel. You experience Joy, Love, Hope, Peace of Mind - A Sense of Well-Being. You are able to successfully cope with the stress and tension of everyday living.

--- When you feel Uncomfortable, you don't like the way you feel. You experience Anger, Fear, or Sadness. You do not have the power to function effectively.

Why Choosing "The Write Way" To Release Your Angry, Sad, Anxious Feeling Is The Right
   Way To Go

   -- It's the way to immediately relieve Inner Tension.

   -- Angry, Sad, Anxious Feelings prevent You from Feeling Good About Yourself.

   -- The sooner you write out your Angry, Sad, Anxious Feelings, the better You will Feel.

   -- You can write out Angry, Sad, Anxious Feelings at any time of day or night. You just
      need pen and paper and the Helping Hand below your wrist.

BE YOUR OWN BEST PEN PAL!!!

THE WRITE WAY TO RELEASE THE FEELING OF ANGER

--- ANGER is Feeling

   agitated, aggravated, annoyed, cheated, disagreeable, discontented, displeased, exasperated, frustrated, hateful, impatient, irritated, outraged, resentful.

--- Write a letter. Write about any experience that caused you to feel Angry.

   -- Use the words or words that best describe your Angry Feelings.

   -- Indicate, specifically, when, where, and what happened.
   -- I felt _____ when _____

   _____
   _____
   _____
   _____
   _____
   _____
   _____
   _____

--- After writing your letter, tear it up and throw it away. The letter has served its purpose. You have gotten rid of your Angry Feelings and made room for Good Feelings and Pleasant Thoughts.

--- Writing out your Angry Feelings before going to sleep allows your Body and Mind to relax, rest comfortably, and recharge itself with Positive Energy.

--- Regardless of the weather outside, you will rise and shine and be able to positively face the new day.

Note: Before tearing up your letter, use the Tally Sheet for GETTING IN TOUCH WITH YOUR ANGRY FEELINGS THROUGH YOUR "t-bars" and your "i-dots" to see how well you score.

WINNING WAYS TO RELIEVE ANGRY FEELINGS

--- Take yourself to a quiet private place. You need space and time to cool down.

--- Listen to soothing music.

--- Whistle or hum a favorite tune. Sing, dance, or play an instrument.

--- Read a book of jokes, puns, riddles, rhymes, tongue twisters.

--- Think of a funny situation that can bring on a smile or laugh.

--- Draw a picture.

--- Look at pictures of favorite people and places.

--- Write a letter to a person you would like to see or talk to. The letter does not require mailing.

--- Take a walk and enjoy the wonders of nature.

THE WRITE WAY TO REDUCE THE FEELING OF FEAR

--- Fear is Feeling
anxious, frightened, intimidated, inhibited, jittery, nervous, overwhelmed, panicky, petrified, pressured, scared, terrified, uptight, worried.

--- Write about what causes You to have Fearful Feelings.

--- State at least 3 steps you can take to handle the situation, should that Fear come to be.
    -- I can

_____
_____
_____

    -- I can

_____
_____
_____

    -- I can

_____
_____
_____

--- Place your Statements in an envelope.

--- Store your Statements in a safe place.

--- Refer to the envelope whenever the event happens.

The Only Fear You Have To Fear, Is The Fear Of Fear.

THE WRITE WAY TO RELIEVE WORRY - ANXIETY - STRESS - TENSION

--- Write a WASTE List
  -- List all the thoughts that are presently creating Worry, Anxiety, Stress, and Tension Energy in your life.
  -- Date the page for some time in the future.
  -- Store the thoughts in a drawer or box - not to be read or thought about until the date specified on the page.
  -- On the specified date, open and read your list of Worries, Anxieties, Stresses and Tensions.

--- How many "What ifs" ever happened?

--- Conclusions:
  -- It is important to deal with one day at a time.
  -- It is impossible to change anything that has already happened.
  -- It is impossible to predict the future. It is a waste of energy to worry about something that may never happen.
  -- Your Brain is designed to deal with one thing at a time. To do otherwise, creates self-confusion.
  -- Deal with the present.
  -- Assume responsibility for the only thing you can change and control. That is -- Yourself- your thoughts, your attitude, your feelings, your actions, your reactions.

WINNING WAYS TO HELP DOUBT AND FEAR TO DISAPPEAR

--- "What if's" create Doubt and set up a mental block against new ideas.

--- A reassuring response to your fearful "what if" questions.

    -- What if _____ were to happen?

    -- Change the words "what if" to "even if" and complete the following statement.

       Even if _____ were to happen, I can handle it, because I choose to believe that I have the inner strength and power to deal with whatever will come to be.

--- Eliminate the words "no", "not", "never" from your thoughts.

I can not change.	I can change.
I have no hope.	I have hope.
I can never succeed.	I can succeed.

THE POWER OF THE PHRASE "I CAN DO IT!!!"

To be used whenever you want Doubt and Fear to disappear.

    -- Say the words "I can do it!" at least 5 times.

    -- Increase your voice volume each time you say the words.

    -- Conclude by quickly raising your arm in mid-air, smiling, and uttering the word "yes"!!

    -- Your Power is reinforced by the height of your arm movement and the broadness of your smile.

THE WRITE WAY TO RELIEVE SADNESS

-- Sadness is Feeling
   alone, betrayed, bitter, bored, confused, crushed, defeated, depressed, devastated, disappointed, discouraged, disgusted, downcast, downhearted, exhausted, fatigued, gloomy, helpless, hopeless, isolated, lonely, overlooked, pessimistic, powerless, rejected, unloved, victimized, worthless.

-- Write about what makes You feel Sad. Use the word or words that best describe your Sadness.

   -- I feel _____ when I remember
      (who, when, where, what happened)

_____
_____
_____
_____
_____
_____
_____
_____
_____
_____

Note:

   -- Long, strong evenly balanced t-bars, slanted upwards will encourage Optimism and Enthusiasm.

THE WRITE WAY TO RELEASE MUSCLE TENSION

--- Curves are tension-free strokes.

    -- Write a series of figure "8's", in slow motion, moving from the left to the right side of the page.

    -- Turn the figure "8" on its side and you have the symbol for eternal life - serenity, harmony.

    -- Loosen up with a series of wide looped "e's" and "l's" Combine the shapes into varying patterns. Use blue or green ink.

    -- Doodle cartoons that focus on curves and circles. Create animals from circle shaped letters of the alphabet. Create heads, features, facial expressions using curved, rounded shapes.

THE WRITE WAY TO A POSITIVE SELF-IMAGE AND BELIEF SYSTEM

--- When You have a Positive Self-Image and Belief System, You have the power and energy to form healthy relationships and function effectively in challenging situations.

--- Use the Simplified Printed "I" for all your written "I" Statements.
    -- A simple, single, straight, vertical downstroke.

--- Do You Know

    -- The Personal Pronoun "I" is the only one letter word that represents the One most important Individual in the world.

    -- The Personal Pronoun "I" is the only Pronoun that is always Capitalized. Capital letters are always used to signify importance.

THE WRITE WAY TO BE THE "I" YOU WANT TO BE

--- You are what you feel.   --- I feel that I am a winner!

--- You believe what you feel.   --- I believe that I am a winner!

--- You are what you believe.   --- I am a winner!

--- From the <u>Glossary Of Positive Adjectives</u>, choose 5 positive adjectives that describe the "I" you want to be.

--- For each word selected, complete the following 3 statements.
        -- I feel that I am _____.
        -- I believe that I am _____.
        -- I am _____.

--- Write and say each set of 3 statements, 3 times each, every day for at least 30 consecutive days.

--- Say the Statements to yourself any time you want to Feel Good about Yourself.

--- It takes at least 30 consecutive days to successfully program your Positive Statements into your Memory Data Bank.

--- After 30 consecutive days, select another 5 adjectives and repeat the Programming Process. There is no limit to the number of adjectives that you may wish to include in your Belief System.

YOU ARE WHO YOU BELIEVE YOU ARE!!!

--- Reminder:
        -- It makes a difference where and how you cross your t-bars.
        -- Place the long, strong, evenly balanced t-bar close to the top of the t-stem.

GLOSSARY OF POSITIVE ADJECTIVES

A --- agreeable alert ambitious amiable

B --- beautiful brainy brave bright brilliant

C --- calm capable careful caring cautious charitable charming cheerful clever competent
confident conscientious considerate contented cooperative courageous

D --- dedicated delightful determined dramatic dynamic

E --- eager energetic enthusiastic

F --- faithful fantastic flexible forgiving friendly

G --- generous gentle great

H --- handsome happy helpful healthy honorable

I --- inquisitive intelligent interesting

J --- jolly jovial joyful jubilant

K --- kind knowledgeable

L --- lively lovable loyal

M --- magnificent marvelous mighty mild-mannered moral

N --- neat neighborly

O --- optimistic outstanding

P --- patient peaceful pleasant polite proud

R -- reasonable receptive relaxed reliable respectful responsible

S --- satisfied secure sincere strong successful

T --- talented thoughtful tolerant trustworthy truthful

U --- understanding unique unselfish

V --- vibrant victorious vigorous vivacious

W --- willing witty wonderful

THE WRITE WAY TO A POSITIVE BELIEF SYSTEM

--- Start a Personal Daily Journal.

--- Date each entry.

--- Make an entry every day.

--- Choose from "I" Winning STATEMENTS FOR POSITIVE ENERGY, those Thoughts that you want to have in your Positive Belief System.

--- Select 5 Thoughts at a time.

--- WRITE - READ - SAY the 5 Thoughts, 3 times each, for 30 days.

--- Use the simplified Printed "I" for all "I" Statements.

--- Every 30 days, choose another 5 Thoughts to add to your entry.

--- Continue to increase the number of Thoughts so that the writing exercise lasts for 20/30 minutes.

--- Writing is a relaxing form of exercise.

--- Effective programming time for written journal entries is shortly before going to sleep.

POSITIVE THOUGHTS PROVIDE POSITIVE ENERGY POWER!!!

"I" STATEMENTS FOR POSITIVE ENERGY POWER

--- I am the only one who is responsible for my thoughts and behavior.
--- I am proud of myself.
--- I am at peace with myself.
--- I am comfortable with myself.
--- I am consistent.
--- I am decisive.
--- I am a good listener.
--- I am in control of what passes my lips--food going in and words coming out.
-- I am unique.

--- I aim to be the best that I can be.

--- I appreciate all the good things that I can do.

--- I believe in myself.
--- I believe in my ability to achieve my goals.
--- I believe that I have the courage and inner strength to get through difficult times.
--- I believe that I am an important Individual.
--- I believe that I count.
--- I believe that I am a winner.
--- I believe that I am a good and deserving person.
--- I believe that I am a success.
--- I believe that I can do anything that I make up my mind to do.
--- I believe that I have the power to solve my problems.

--- I hold no grudges.

--- I know there are at least two alternatives to every situation--a positive one, and a negative one.

--- I learn and grow from my mistakes.
--- I like who I am.
--- I respect myself.
--- I take good care of myself.

--- I value myself.

WINNING WAYS TO FEEL GOOD

     THE POWER OF JOURNALING

     MODERATE EXERCISE

     THE COMFORT OF A HUG

     PICTURE VISUALIZATION

     POINTER-CISE

     VOWEL SOUND COUNT-OUT

     ACTS OF KINDNESS

THE POWER OF JOURNALING

-- Start a Journal of Pleasant Memories
-- Make daily entries.
-- Date each entry.

-- Write about one or more events that made you feel that you had a Great Day.

-- Indicate specifically - when, where, and what happened.

-- Writing in your Journal before going to sleep is a relaxing activity and is the right way to go for pleasant dreams.

-- Read your Journal whenever you want to refresh your Memory and relive happy, exciting events. It's guaranteed to keep you smiling.

-- Share your Journal of Pleasant Memories with others.

--- MODERATE EXERCISE -- MODERATE IN FREQUENCY AND DURATION

   -- Increases the Blood and Oxygen Supply to your Heart and Lungs.

   -- Lowers the level of Carbon Dioxide in your Lungs.

   -- Lowers your Blood Pressure.

   -- Relieves your Muscle Tension.

   -- Increases your Metabolic Efficiency.

   -- Improves your Learning Capacity.

   -- Improves your Mood and ability to handle stressful situations.

   -- Select an activity that you feel you will enjoy.
        -- a 10 - 30 minute brisk walk, swimming, dancing, bicycling, yoga, tai-chi

   -- Seek a place that offers you fresh air, sunshine, peace, and tranquility.

--- Do You Know

   -- When you sweat, you are getting rid of harmful chemicals.

--- THE COMFORT OF A HUG -- A SIMPLE PAIN-FREE WORKOUT

    -- Aches and Pains need the Comfort of a Hug.

    -- Extending your arms instantly releases Muscle Tension.

    -- Give and get at least one Hug each day.

    -- If no one is available, Hug yourself.

--- PICTURE VISUALIZATION

-- Enjoy the Spring Season all year round.

--- Surround yourself with pictures, posters, paintings, of scenes that celebrate Spring -- the Season of Renewal, Harmony, Peace, Hope, and Joy.

-- Visualize yourself within the setting.
-- Observe the Colors. Listen to the Sounds. Smell the Scents.

-- For Pleasant Dreams, view the picture/ poster before going to sleep.

-- To have a great day, view the picture /poster upon waking.

POINTER -CISE TO POSITIVELY ENERGIZE

--- A simple exercise routine that is guaranteed to generate physical and emotional fitness, flexibility, balance, and high Self-Esteem.

--- Physical examination is not required prior to Pointer-cising. There are no physical restrictions, limitations, side effects, or risks.

--- When?
> Number and length of daily sessions depends upon your need throughout each day.

--- Where?
> Pointer-cising can be done in a standing, sitting, or reclining position. Your comfort is the determining factor.

--- What equipment is needed?
-- Your favored Pointer Finger, of either your right or left hand.
-- "I" Winning Statements For Positive Energy.

--- Pointer-cising Routine
1. Select one or more statement from "I" Winning Statements For Positive Energy.
2. Bend your elbow and face the palm side of your hand.
3. Straighten your Pointer Finger. Relax all other fingers.
4. Each statement begins with the Letter "I". Your straight Pointer represents that word.
5. Bend your Pointer Finger and point to yourself as you say the remaining words in the statement.
6. Return Pointer to a straight position at the end of the statement.

--- Choose to say as many statements as many times as you wish.

--- Repeat steps 2-6 each time you say a statement.

--- CPR for successful Pointer-cising
> Commitment - Patience - Practice - Repetition - Reinforcement

--- For added fun, and pleasure when Pointer-cising
- Draw a smile on your Pointer. (2 dots and a curve)
- Place a Smile Sticker on your Pointer.
- Say your "I" Statements in front of a mirror.
- Add "yes" or "yes, I believe" before each statement.
- Smile and nod your head up and down. Avoid any side to side motion.
- End each Statement with a "thumbs up" signal.

--- Important Reminder:
- Your Pointer always faces you and bends only in your direction.
- Do not use the Pointer in an outward direction. That destructive, fault-finding, accusing, blaming motion aims to hurt, creates an angry, frustrating environment and depletes your Positive Energy Power!!!!

VOWEL SOUND COUNT-OUT

--- Rx - For Defusing Negative Energy - Anger, Fear, Sadness
   -- Restoring Inner Bio-Chemical Balance
   -- Using Deep Breathing and the Vowel Sounds "a", "e", "i", "o", "u"

--- Procedure - Series of 5 Deep Breaths
   -- Step 1 - Silently inhale to the count of 4.
   -- Step 2 - Hold breath for the count of 2.
   -- Step 3 - Audibly exhale to the count of 4, using one Vowel Sound.

   -- Repeat steps 1 - 3, using a different Vowel Sound each time.

   -- The Series of 5 Deep Breaths can be repeated as many times as it takes for your
      Body Systems to cool down.

   -- Use loosely extended fingers for counting.
      -- Left hand fingers for inhale count.
      -- Right hand fingers for exhale count.

   -- 5 Count Version
      -- Step 1 - Silently inhale to the count of 5.
      -- Step 2 - Hold Breath for the count of 2.
      -- Step 3 - Audibly exhale to the count of 5, using each Vowel Sound per count-
         out.

--- It is helpful to visualize the clear, uncluttered shape of the Vowels "a" and "o".

ACTS OF KINDNESS -- A POSITIVE ENERGY PROJECT

--- Reach out and Help Others.
   -- Say a Kind Word. Perform a Kind Deed.

--- Kind Words, Compliments, and Compassion can instantly increase a Person's Positive
   Energy Power (PEP).

--- Earn 2 credits for each time you do an Act of Kindness.
   -- Share a smile.
   -- Hug someone.
   -- Extend a helping hand.
   -- Use the magic words -- "Please" and "Thank You".

--- Keep a Daily Score of Credits Earned.

--- Invite Relatives, Friends, and Classmates to participate in the Acts of Kindness Project.
   -- Share the Weekly Score results.
   -- Be a Weekly Winner.
   -- Choose how to celebrate your successes.
   -- Determine what kind of recognition, rewards, or awards will give pleasure to the
      Weekly Winners with the highest scores.

--- Bonus Acts of Kindness Projects
   -- Set up Kindness Community Projects.
   -- Share the results of your successful projects with other Classes, Schools, Organizations,
      and the News Media,.

Enjoy Your Positive Energy Power - Yes!!!

THE POWER OF SMILES AND LAUGHTER

Laughter is the most inexpensive and most effective wonder drug.
      Laughter is a universal medicine.
                                                      Bertrand Russell

A Mile Of Smiles Each Day Goes A Long Way To Heal What Ails You.
      -- Relaxes your Facial Muscles.
      -- Softens your Frown Lines.
      -- Acts as a Natural Face Lift.

A Laugh A Day Keeps The Stress Away.
      -- Gives your Heart and Diaphragm Muscles a beneficial workout.
      -- Improves your Circulation.
      -- Fills your Lungs with Oxygen-rich air.
      -- Clears your Respiratory Passages.
      -- Stimulates the Release of Endorphins into your Bloodstream. Endorphins are Hormones
         that help you to "feel good".
      -- Reduces the tension in your Central Nervous System.

Laughter is free, legal, has no calories, no cholesterol, no preservatives, no artificial ingredients
      and is absolutely safe.
                                                      Dale Irvin

ALPHA WORD COLLECTIONS - THE WRITE WAY TO MILES OF SMILES AND TONS OF TONGUE TWISTERS

An ALPHA WORD COLLECTION is made up of NOUNS, ADJECTIVES, and ACTION WORDS that start with the same Letter of the Alphabet.

For tons of Tongue Twisters

-- Select one or more Nouns.

-- Add one or more Adjectives that describe the Nouns.

-- Add one or more Action Words that tell what the Noun or Nouns are doing.

-- Say your completed sentences out loud, 3 or more times.

-- Share your Tongue Twisters with others.

Start an Alpha Word Collection of Nouns, Adjectives, and Action Words for every letter of the Alphabet.

To expand the supply of Words for your Tongue Twisters, select and combine Nouns, Adjectives, and Action Words from any Alpha Word Collection.

Note:
--- A Dictionary is the source to use to help your Word Collection grow.

THE "a" WORD COLLECTION OF NOUNS, ADJECTIVES, AND ACTION WORDS
aims at adding an abundance of Tongue Twisters

--- NOUNS

accident ache agreement air airplane airport alarm alligator allowance army animal ant ape apple apron aquarium area adventure ax arm aunt athlete attachment attention attitude autumn award abundance

Alice Andrea Anne Alyson Adeline Amanda Aileen Anita Agatha Amy Ariel Annette Arlene Alexandra Aaron Adam Alvin Albert Anthony Andrew Arthur Adrian Allen Alex

--- Descriptive Words

able abundant adorable affectionate aggressive agreeable alert amused angry active ambitious amiable anxious atrocious attentive attractive awkward awful athletic atrocious automatic

--- Action Words

act add admire agree aim allow alter answer appear are arrive ask attach attack avoid awake ate approve assist appreciate

--- Examples:

-- The active alligator appeared at the airy airport.
-- The amiable ape ate an abundance of awful apples.

THE "d" WORD COLLECTION OF NOUNS, ADJECTIVES, AND ACTION WORDS
definitely does deliver dozens of Tongue Twisters

--- Nouns

Dad dance danger date dateline daughter day decision decoration deed deer degree dentist desk diamond digit dime dinner dinosaur direction directory dirt disappearance discussion disk dog doctor doll dollar dollhouse donkey door dot dragon dream dress drum duck dude dust
Diane Dale Doris Donna Daphne Doreen Danielle Dolores Dana Deborah Daniel Dennis Donald Douglas Drew David

--- Descriptive Words

dangerous daring dark deafening defiant delicious delighted dense desperate determined devoted difficult dim dirty disagreeable discouraged disgusted disliked dissatisfied distant distinct doubtful dozen downhearted downstairs dreadful dreary dry dull durable dusk dusty dynamic

--- Action Words

dance dangle dare dash decide decorate deliver demand deny describe deserve destroy do does did die dig digest disappear discuss dismiss drink draw drive drop drown dump

--- Examples:

-- The determined dog dug dozens of deep, dark ditches.
-- The dynamic dragon danced with the delighted dinosaur.

THE "g" WORD COLLECTION OF NOUNS, ADJECTIVES, AND ACTION WORDS
gives you great Tongue Twisters

--- Nouns

gadget gallon game gang gap garage garden gas gate geese gift giraffe girl gland glare glass globe glove glue goal goat goldfish goose gown grade graduate grain grandmother grandfather grape grass grease ground group guide gum gun
Gail Greta Grace Gladys Gina Gloria Gwen George Gary Gregory Gerard Gerald Gabriel

--- Descriptive Words

generous gentle genuine gigantic glad glamourous gleaming glistening gloomy glorious glossy glowing glum golden good good-natured graceful gracious grainy grand grateful gray greasy great green grim grotesque guilty

--- Action Words

gain gallop gather get give glare glide glisten glow go graduate grant grill grind groan grow growl

--- Examples:

-- The gigantic giraffe galloped to the green, glossy grass.
-- Gary gave Grace a graceful, golden goose.

THE "l" WORD COLLECTION OF NOUNS, ADJECTIVES, AND ACTION WORDS
leads to lively Tongue Twisters

--- Nouns

       ladder lady lake lamb lamp land law leaf leaflet leak leopard leash leather leg lemon lemonade length lens letter library lid life light lime line lion lip list lizzard loaf lock log lunch

       Lisa Laura Lillian Lenore Lauren Linda Lesley Lindsay Louise Leon Larry Leonard Leo Luke Louis Lyle Lorraine Lila

--- Descriptive Words

       large last late lazy least left light little lively lonely lonesome long loose lost loud lovable low lucky

--- Action Words

       laugh lean learn leap leave let lift listen live look lose lead

--- Examples:

       -- The little lizzard and the large leopard like lamb for lunch.
       -- Larry and Lisa lost the last, long, legal letter.

THE "m" WORD COLLECTION OF NOUNS, ADJECTIVES, AND ACTION WORDS
makes for many, merry Tongue Twisters

--- Nouns

machine mail man map mark mat match material meal meat medicine men mice
mile milk minute mistake moment money monkey month morning mother
mountain mouse mouth mud murmur music muzzle
Max Martin Matthew Mark Margaret Megan Minerva Melanie Mitchell Marvin
Marilyn Michelle Millicent Madeline

--- Descriptive Words

magic magnificent many marvelous massive meager mean meek merry metallic
microscopic mighty mild million miniature miserable misty modern moody
motionless muddy

--- Action Words

made march marry may meet melt miss move murmur

--- Examples:

-- The many, mighty men marched many muddy miles.
-- Many merry monkeys made merry music.

THE "t" WORD COLLECTION OF NOUNS, ADJECTIVES, AND ACTION WORDS
tend to lead to tons of Tongue Twisters

--- Nouns

table tag tail tailor tale tank tape tax taxi tea teacup teacher team teenager teaspoon teeth telegram telephone temperature temple tenant tennis tent terrier test textbook thief thimble thorn thought thread throat throne thumb thunder ticket tie tiger time timetable tire title toad toast tobacco toes tomato ton tongue tools tooth toothache toothbrush top tortoise total towel town toys track traffic trailer trail train transfer trap trash traveler tray treat treatment treasure tree trial triangle tribe trick tricycle trip trouble truck trumpet trunk truth tub tube tunnel turkey turn turtle turnpike tusks twig twin twine typewriter
Tyrannosaurus
Thomas Terry Tina Timothy Theresa Theodore Thelma

--- Descriptive Words

talkative tall tame tan tasteless tasty tearful temporary ten tender tense terrible terrific terrified the their these thick thin third thirsty thirteen thirty this those thoughtful thousand three thousandth thrilled thunderous tidy tight timid tiny tired tolerant tough towering tragic trivial tremendous triumphant troubled trustworthy truthful twelve twelfth twentieth twenty two

--- Action Words

take talk tangle tap tape taste teach tear tease tell test thank think throw thump tickle tie toss touch train transfer treasure travel treat tremble trip trim trust try tumble turn twist

--- Examples:
  -- Thirty-two teenagers took ten tough tests.
  -- Ten tigers took turns talking to twenty-two trembling terriers.

Smiles and Laughter are meant to be shared.

Highly Recommended -- THE HEALTHY HUMOR PROJECT

Write and Self-Publish an annual edition of <u>LAUGH YOUR WAY TO GOOD HEALTH</u> a Collection of Tongue Twisters, Rhymes, and Riddles.

Share your Book with Children in Hospitals. It is guaranteed to help them to heal!!!

Bibliography

Amend,Karen & Ruiz,Mary S.. *Handwriting Analysis*.
    North Hollywood, California: Newcastle Publishing Co. Inc., 1980

De Sainte Colombe, Paul, *Grapho-Therarpeutics: Pen and Pencil Therapy*.
    Hollywood, California: Laurida Books Publishing Co., 1966

Gardner, Ruth, *Instant Handwriting Analysis*
    St. Paul, Minnesota: Llewellyn Publications Inc., 1989

Grayson, David, *Better Understanding Your Child Through Handwriting*
    LaGrange, Illinois: GBC Publishing, 1981

Holder, Robert, *You Can Analyze Handwriting*
    Englewood Cliffs, N.J.: Prentice Hall, Inc. 1958

Hollander, P. Scott, *Reading Between The Lines*
    St. Paul, Minnesota: Llewellyn Publications Inc., 1991

Lindberg, Elayne,V., *The Power of Positive Handwriting*
    Staples, Minnesota: Adventure Publications, 1989

Marcuse, Irene, *Guide To Personality Through Your Handwriting*
    New York,: ARC Books Inc., Second Edition, 1967

McNichol, Andrea and Nelson. Jeffrey A.*, Handwriting Analysis. Putting It To
        Work For You*
    Chicago, Ill.: Contemporary Books, 1991

Roman, Klara G.*, Encyclopedia of the Written Word*
    New York: Frederick Ungar Publishing Co., 1968

Bibliography

Amend,Karen & Ruiz,Mary S.. *Handwriting Analysis*.
    North Hollywood, California: Newcastle Publishing Co. Inc., 1980

De Sainte Colombe, Paul, *Grapho-Therarpeutics: Pen and Pencil Therapy*.
    Hollywood, California: Laurida Books Publishing Co., 1966

Gardner, Ruth, *Instant Handwriting Analysis*
    St. Paul, Minnesota: Llewellyn Publications Inc., 1989

Grayson, David, *Better Understanding Your Child Through Handwriting*
    LaGrange, Illinois: GBC Publishing, 1981

Holder, Robert, *You Can Analyze Handwriting*
    Englewood Cliffs, N.J.: Prentice Hall, Inc. 1958

Hollander, P. Scott, *Reading Between The Lines*
    St. Paul, Minnesota: Llewellyn Publications Inc., 1991

Lindberg, Elayne,V., *The Power of Positive Handwriting*
    Staples, Minnesota: Adventure Publications, 1989

Marcuse, Irene, *Guide To Personality Through Your Handwriting*
    New York,: ARC Books Inc., Second Edition, 1967

McNichol, Andrea and Nelson. Jeffrey A., *Handwriting Analysis. Putting It To
        Work For You*
    Chicago, Ill.: Contemporary Books, 1991

Roman, Klara G., *Encyclopedia of the Written Word*
    New York: Frederick Ungar Publishing Co., 1968

Smiles and Laughter are meant to be shared.

Highly Recommended -- THE HEALTHY HUMOR PROJECT

Write and Self-Publish an annual edition of <u>LAUGH YOUR WAY TO GOOD HEALTH</u> a
Collection of Tongue Twisters, Rhymes, and Riddles.

Share your Book with Children in Hospitals. It is guaranteed to help them to heal!!!

Santoy, Claude, Ph.D., *Write What's Wrong*
N.Y.: Paragon House, 1992
The ABCs of Handwriting Analysis
N.Y.: Paragon House, 1989
Interpreting Your Child's Handwriting and Drawings:
Toddler to Teen
N.Y.:   Paragon House, 1991

Sara, Dorothy, *Handwriting Analysis for the Millions*.
N.Y. :Bell Publishing Co., 1967

Singer, Eric, *Personality in Handwriting*
Wesport, Ct.; Associated Booksellers, 1954

Stoller, Richard, J. Ph.D.,   *Write Right: Change Your Writing to Change*
Your Life, 1978
The Psychology of Penmanship. 1993

www.ingramcontent.com/pod-product-compliance
Lightning Source LLC
Chambersburg PA
CBHW081221280526
45787CB00006B/2473